HOW TO MAKE
OVER 200 COCKTAILS

HOW TO MAKE OVER 200 COCKTAILS

Margaret Barca

CLAREMONT BOOKS

PENGUIN BOOKS

Published by the Penguin Group
Penguin Books Ltd, 27 Wrights Lane, London W8 5TZ, England
Penguin Books USA Inc., 375 Hudson Street, New York, New York 10014, USA
Penguin Books Australia Ltd, Ringwood, Victoria, Australia
Penguin Books Canada Ltd, 10 Alcorn Avenue, Toronto, Ontario, Canada M4V 3B2
Penguin Books (NZ) Ltd, 182–190 Wairau Road, Auckland 10, New Zealand

Penguin Books Ltd, Registered Offices: Harmondsworth, Middlesex, England

First published by Penguin Books 1991
Reprinted with minor revisions 1994

This edition published by Claremont Books,
an imprint of Godfrey Cave Associates Limited,
42 Bloomsbury Street, London WC1B 3QJ,
under licence from Penguin Books Ltd, 1995

ISBN 1 85471 762 6

CONTENTS

INTRODUCTION

Strictly speaking, a cocktail is defined as a short, dry aperitif; a potent drink with a spirit base, correctly served before dinner to whet the appetite. But that is very strictly speaking, for a cocktail is now generally understood to be any mixed drink, often exotically coloured, resplendent with decoration and served any time of the day (or night).

The cocktail's history is surprisingly long, with a printed mention of cocktails as early as 1806 in an American magazine. It was during the Prohibition era in the States, however, that cocktails enjoyed enormous popularity. In the 1920s and 1930s, a dash of this and a dash of that was used to disguise (and improve) an often hefty dose of illicit alcohol. And, swept up in the spirit of the Jazz Age, cocktails became synonymous with glamour and good times, an image that still lingers.

In *How to Make Over 200 Cocktails* we give you a selection of the classics, from a Martini and a Manhattan to many of today's most fashionable mixed drinks, often with a vodka or tequila base, tropical fruits and all manner of colourful liqueurs. After sampling some of these, you may even be inspired to invent your own cocktail.

Here's cheers!

HOW TO USE THIS BOOK

Recipes for cocktails are listed in alphabetical order. The Index lists cocktails under the base spirit and main alcoholic ingredients.

A symbol beside each recipe indicates the type of serving glass suggested (see *GLASSES* on page 7 for key to symbols).

Non-alcoholic cocktails are indicated by an asterisk beside the heading.

Cross references to other sections, headings within sections and recipes are indicated throughout the text by *ITALIC SMALL CAPITAL LETTERS*.

All recipes are for 1 serving, unless otherwise specified.

EQUIPMENT

The best cocktails are prepared with a certain degree of finesse and served with a flourish.

To shake, stir, strain, slice, swizzle and serve in style you need the right equipment. While bowls, knives and blenders are standard kitchen equipment, you should be able to find anything else you need in specialist shops or department stores.

If you are buying a specific item, invest in quality. An elegant cocktail shaker or a beautiful glass jug adds just that much more fun to cocktail making.

blender Not as romantic as a cocktail shaker perhaps, but perfect for those creamy, fruity cocktails that are best served frothy. If the blender doesn't have specially strengthened blades, use crushed ice, not cubes.

bottle opener The 'bartender's friend' is preferred by professionals as it can peel away wrapping from a bottle, open a can or bottle and pull a cork. Those who feel their wrists are a little weak might prefer a more elaborate corkscrew, which demands less effort.

bowls For cocktail cherries, olives and other garnishes.

chopping board, citrus peeler, paring knife, zester For professional garnishes. Keep everything scrupulously clean, and the knife razor sharp. A citrus peeler (illustrated) is very useful for cutting thin spirals of peel.

grater For grating nutmeg or chocolate for garnishes.

ice-bucket Plenty of ice is needed so make sure you have a generous-sized container. A lidded bucket helps keep the ice for longer.

ice-crusher A luxury it's true, and probably only for the dedicated cocktail bartender.

ice-scoop Ideal for loading ice into a glass or cocktail shaker.

ice tongs Allow you to clink individual blocks into a glass without extra water (and are also very good for handling fruit garnishes).

jug Generous in size, preferably glass, and with a lip to hold back ice.

juice extractor Perfect for fresh fruit cocktails. If you don't have an extractor, you will need a simple lemon juice squeezer.

knives see *CHOPPING BOARD*

measures A double-ended measure is practical; 15 millilitres (ml), 25 ml and 30 ml are common (see MEASURES on page 20). A pourer that fits on the top of a bottle (sometimes called a jigger) is excellent for frequently used spirits like gin or brandy.

mixing glass For drinks that are stirred. This item is like a jug without a handle, and is large enough to mix several cocktails at once.

muddler Used to crush sugar or bruise fresh mint leaves, for example, in the glass. It looks like a swizzle stick with a bulbous end.

shaker The classic cocktail shaker comes in three pieces, with a strainer in the top. Most are stainless steel or silver. The 'Boston' shaker has metal and glass sections, but no strainer. Never fill your shaker to the top and always ensure it is securely closed.

soda siphon Another professional touch. If you want just a 'squirt' of soda water, this saves opening a bottle. It also helps make drinks that should fizz do just that.

spoons A long-handled barspoon for stirring drinks. A tablespoon and teaspoon are practical for measuring.

strainer Either the classic 'Hawthorne' strainer or one of the practical clip-on varieties.

other equipment For those final flourishes: swizzle sticks, straws, toothpicks, paper napkins, and decorations, such as tiny paper umbrellas (see also GARNISHES).

GLASSES

Presentation of your cocktail is critical. Glasses should be carefully washed and rinsed, wiped and then polished with a lint-free cloth.

To chill the glass before filling, place it in the refrigerator or freezer for a few minutes, or swish with ice before polishing.

Classic drinks are usually served in classic-shaped glasses. The symbol next to each recipe suggests the type of glass you might use, but the final decision is yours.

balloon or goblet (holds 150–200 ml). Like a giant brandy snifter. The generous size makes it just right for frothy, heavily garnished concoctions and some of the beautifully coloured modern cocktails.

champagne flute (about 150 ml) Perfect for simple but sophisticated cocktails, especially those using wine or champagne.

champagne saucer (about 140 ml) No longer in vogue for fine champagne, as the sparkle is so quickly lost, but an elegant shape for many of the creamy, frothy short cocktails.

cocktail (about 90 ml) The classic Martini glass, triangular in shape, usually used for short, strong drinks and aperitifs. The stem ensures your hand doesn't warm the drink.

highball (200–285 ml) A tall straight-sided glass for long cool drinks, as well as soft drinks and beer. The tallest version is sometimes called a 'Collins'.

liqueur (30–60 ml) A small stemmed glass for serving rich liqueurs.

old fashioned (120–125 ml) Short, business-like glass for drinks served 'on the rocks', sometimes whisky or fruit juice.

pilsener (210–300 ml) Tall, V-shaped glass, very effective for drinks mixed with beer, stout or lemonade.

toddy (200–250 ml) Heatproof glass with handle, best for serving hot toddies, egg nog, mulled wine or any of the numerous coffees laced with liqueurs.

wine glasses (140–180 ml) Available in countless shapes. Generally, the white wine glass is slightly slimmer and smaller than the red wine glass.

STOCKING THE BAR

As a basis you will need a good dry **gin**, a clear **vodka** and a reasonable quality **brandy**. A light (or 'white'), a gold and a dark **rum** would stand you in good stead, but if your budget doesn't stretch to that, a rum such as Bacardi Light Rum is probably the most versatile.

As for **whisky**, there is no need to use an expensive brand of Scotch whisky; any whisky and a bourbon are fine for mixing. Use Scotch whisky when specified, but save your very best Scotch to serve straight or on the rocks.

Tequila, the base of many newer cocktails is well worth stocking.

Vermouth (sweet and dry) and **Campari** are two of the best aperitifs for mixing.

Liqueurs might include **cognac, Cointreau, Kahlua, Grand Marnier, maraschino, Tia Maria,** a **curaçao, crème de menthe, crème de cassis** and perhaps **Galliano**.

And, naturally, every bar should have some **champagne**.

This sounds a heady – and long – list. But of course you don't have to buy full-size (750 ml) bottles. Half-bottles of spirits and liqueurs (and even sample bottles) are practical, especially while you are still experimenting.

BASICS FOR THE BAR

A bottle of **Angostura bitters** is essential, though a well-equipped bar will also have the drier **orange bitters**. **Grenadine**, a sweet pomegranate-flavoured syrup, is another must-have. **Gomme**, a sugar syrup that makes sweetening drinks simple, can be bought but it is easy to make your own.

To make your own **sugar syrup**: heat 1 cup of water with 1 cup of sugar. Bring to the boil while stirring, then simmer gently until the sugar is dissolved. Cool and keep refrigerated in a corked bottle.

You should also have some powdered or **castor sugar**. This dissolves quickly at low temperatures when mixed with alcohol and is needed to sugar-frost glasses (see GARNISHES on page 16). **Salt** is needed for flavouring and for salt-frosting glasses, and pepper adds flavour to drinks like a BLOODY MARY. It may be worth keeping some hot Tabasco sauce and a bottle of spicy Worcestershire sauce in your bar as these are essential ingredients for some excellent 'pick-me-up' drinks. **Nutmeg** and **cinnamon** are worth stocking as garnishes.

You will need a supply of **soft drinks** (soda water, lemonade, dry ginger ale, bitter lemon) and fruit juices (orange, pineapple and tomato are popular).

Cream and **milk** are needed if you will be serving some of the fashionable creamy cocktails. UHT long-life cream and milk are handy to have as a standby. Coconut cream (available at most supermarkets) is also worth keeping.

For garnishes and 'a twist of', have a supply of **limes**, **lemons** and **oranges**, and fresh fruit (such as strawberries and pineapple) and **fresh mint**. **Cocktail cherries** and **olives** are frequently called for.

HOW TO MAKE THE PERFECT COCKTAIL

There is an art to cocktail making. It is more than just the ingredients – it is the manner in which the ingredients are put together and served.

'Stirred not shaken, shaken but not rocked to sleep.' Cocktail drinkers can be *very* particular, so here are some essential terms to recognise and simple techniques to master.

blend Place the ingredients into an electric blender, add crushed ice and blend until smooth. Cocktails with fruit, cream and eggs are usually blended.

build Pour the ingredients directly into the glass, one on top of the other.

float There are two techniques and experts disagree about which is the most successful. Pour the liquid very slowly over the back of a spoon so that it slides into the glass and floats on top. Alternatively, pour the liquid into the bowl of the spoon, allowing it to gradually spill onto the drink's surface as the spoon fills.

frost See GARNISHES for how to sugar- or salt-frost glasses.

muddle Using a muddler (which is like a swizzle stick with a bulbous end), or the wrong end of a barspoon, crush sugar and other ingredients in the base of a glass.

shake Fill your cocktail shaker with ice cubes (if specified), pour in the ingredients, secure the top and shake. But not for too long. A short, sharp action – up and down – is best. Then strain the cocktail into a glass immediately. If you wait too long the ice will dilute the drink.

stir Many of the classic cocktails are stirred. Pour the ingredients into a mixing glass, stir with ice until just chilled, then strain into a glass.

twist Take a small piece of clean lemon peel, hold it over the drink and twist gently to release a few drops of natural oil, adding a subtle flavour and aroma to the drink. It is usual to then drop the peel into the cocktail.

ICE

Ice is an essential part of cocktail making, so always ensure you have a fresh, clean supply.

Ice cubes are usually used in a shaker or mixing glass to chill a drink. Strain your drink then add fresh ice if needed. Spray a little soda water on ice cubes in a bucket to stop them sticking together.

For *frappés* and some long drinks that require a blender, crushed ice is usually used. If you don't have an ice-crusher, wrap cubes in a clean tea-towel and hit with a kitchen mallet to break (noisy but effective).

Ice cubes made in distinctive shapes (for example

stars, diamonds) can add to your cocktail. When making ice cubes, add slivers of lemon or orange, fresh mint leaves or borage flowers for an unusual garnish.

HINTS

- Always buy good quality ingredients. And don't buy the cheapest spirits – they can ruin a cocktail.

- Keep everything spotlessly clean.

- Keep glasses washed and polished. Handle by the stem or base so that you don't heat the glass or leave fingerprints. And chill the glass before pouring in the cocktail.

- Make sure you have plenty of fresh, clean ice.

- Refrigerate garnishes or keep them on ice.

- If an egg is called for, break it into a separate glass first, to ensure it is fresh.

- Serve your cocktails as soon as they are made. Cocktails with egg and cream can separate. Drinks with ice can become too diluted.

- Always offer non-alcoholic cocktails for those guests who prefer not to drink alcohol.

GARNISHES

How your cocktail looks is *almost* as important as how it tastes, and how it looks depends on how you garnish.

There are two schools of thought – the minimal (a cherry, if you must) and the exotic (fight your way to your drink!). Somewhere in between is probably the ideal. Just remember – the garnish should add to the drink, not detract from it.

CITRUS FRUITS

Lemon, lime and orange are the basic essentials. The fruit should be fresh, unblemished and is best if washed just before serving. If you prepare fruit beforehand, keep it covered in the refrigerator or on ice.

fruit rings If the ring is to float in the glass, cut a fairly thin slice of fruit. If a segment is to rest on the rim of the glass, a chunkier piece will sit more easily.

a knot Slice a long thin strip of peel. Tie gently and drop into the drink.

spiced fruit A half slice of lemon or orange studded with cloves is ideal for mulled wine or a hot toddy.

A spiral Using a sharp paring knife or vegetable peeler, cut the peel by moving around the fruit in one continuous strip. Do not cut the bitter white pith.

twisted rings Use a toothpick to hold rings in an 'S' shape. Use different fruits (for example lime and orange) for effect. Spear a cherry on the toothpick as well, for extra colour.

VARIOUS FRUIT SUGGESTIONS

banana Fun to decorate some of the tropical cocktail concoctions. Choose firm, pale fruit without marks. Don't peel the banana, cut thick slices and dip in fresh lemon juice to prevent browning before using.

cherries Maraschino or cocktail cherries come in a range of colours (even blue!). They can float on top of a cocktail, rest on the rim of the glass or be speared, singly or in clusters, on a toothpick and balanced across the glass. Alternatively, fresh cherries can be hung over the rim of the glass.

kiwi fruit Cut in rings or lengthwise wedges and place on the rim of the glass.

melon Fresh cantaloup or honeydew melon scooped into balls and speared on a toothpick is sometimes suggested for tropical drinks.

pineapple Excellent for long cocktails served in generously-sized glasses. Cut triangles or long spear-shaped wedges. Secure a cherry, strawberry and/or sprig of fresh mint leaves to a piece of pineapple with a toothpick. For fruity drinks.

strawberries Wash well before using, as they can be gritty. Make a small slit and place on the rim of the glass, or cut several times to create a fan effect.

OTHER GARNISHES

cucumber Scrub the skin well and cut long sticks of cucumber or thin spirals of peel: perfect for long cool drinks like Pimm's.

fresh mint Attach a sprig of mint leaves with a toothpick to a citrus slice, a strawberry or other fruit.

TOPPINGS

For creamy cocktails (like *BRANDY ALEXANDER*), try a dusting of freshly grated nutmeg or powdered cinnamon.

Liqueur coffees, such as *MEXICAN COFFEE* (see *IRISH COFFEE*), could have freshly grated chocolate sprinkled on the cream.

FROSTING

Frosting gives your drinks a professional finish. It is best done on the traditional cocktail-shaped glass. Hold the glass by the stem and dip it into lemon juice (or rub a piece of lemon around the rim). Then spread salt or sugar (depending on whether the drink is sweet or not) evenly on a small plate and dip the rim into this, giving it a small twist. The sugar or salt will adhere. You can also dip the rim into orange juice or one of the syrups, such as blackcurrant or grenadine, which will create a mar-vellous coloured rim. Or, for a sweeter frosting, dip the glass in lightly beaten egg white. Do not try to frost the glass using water – the sugar or salt will dissolve.

MEASUREMENTS

Measurements for recipes in this book are given in millilitres (ml). Double-ended cocktail measures are often 15 ml and 30 ml, the standard measure used in cocktails being 25 to 30 ml, or slightly less than one fluid ounce. Below is a short liquid measure conversion table, followed by a table listing some of the terms you may encounter when making (and discussing) cocktails.

Liquid Measures

$\frac{1}{8}$ fl oz = 3.5 ml	1 fl oz = 28.5 ml
$\frac{1}{4}$ fl oz = 7 ml	$1\frac{1}{2}$ fl oz = 43 ml
$\frac{1}{2}$ fl oz = 14 ml	2 fl oz = 57 ml

Traditional Measures

dash	About 10 drops, or a quick shake of the bottle	
gill	142 ml	5 fl oz
pint	568 ml	20 fl oz

THE MORNING AFTER

The soundest advice is, of course, not to over-indulge. Cocktails are very potent drinks and should always be consumed responsibly and in moderation, and if you drink, don't drive. However, if you don't have to travel anywhere you may be tempted towards the tipsy stage. In which case, it's probably worth thinking about the 'morning after' the night before.

Before you begin celebrating – and there is always *something* worth celebrating – drink a glass of milk. It will help line your stomach and slow down the absorption of alcohol.

After celebrating, but *before* retiring for the night, drink as many glasses of water as you can. This helps counteract the dehydration that alcohol causes, which can make you feel so ghastly.

Rest is always a good cure (though not always achievable). If you can, keep your head under the bedclothes for as long as possible.

Some people swear by vitamin C. Others firmly believe in vitamin B1. Well, it's worth a try. In most cases you couldn't do yourself any more harm.

The Italians serve a measure of the powerful bitter digestive Fernet Branca with soda water as a restorative.

Or you might try a few dashes of Angostura bitters in soda water. Just sip it slowly.

Many claim the 'hair of the dog' is the only cure, but let's face it – that is what caused the trouble in the first place.

A *BLOODY MARY*, combining a stiff enough dash of alcohol with a respectable quantity of nutritious tomato juice, is sometimes recommended.

There are those who would advocate a drink called a *BULLSHOT*, containing beef bouillon, but if you can drink soup in your condition, perhaps you aren't that sick anyway.

Finally, the following recipe for a Prairie Hen may do the trick (if it doesn't do you in altogether!). Experts suggest you close your eyes as you drink.

PRAIRIE HEN

5 ml vinegar
10 ml Worcestershire sauce
2 dashes of Tabasco sauce
1 egg (do not break the yolk)
salt and pepper

Pour into an old-fashioned glass and drink.

GLOSSARY

advocaat A rich, creamy Dutch liqueur made from eggs, sugar and brandy, golden in colour. Cherry advocaat has cherry brandy added.

amaretto An amber-coloured Italian liqueur with a nutty apricot flavour, reputedly first made near Lake Como in northern Italy in about 1525.

Amer Picon Syrupy French aperitif, flavoured with a mixture of orange and aromatic herbs.

Angostura bitters The best known of the aromatic bitters, a blend of herbs and spices first produced in 1824 in Venezuela as a medicinal preparation. Although only used in minute quantities in each drink, it is indispensable in the cocktail cabinet. Other bitters worth seeking out are orange bitters and Peychaud bitters.

anisette Sweetened aniseed liqueur with a pure spirit base. Produced commercially in the French Bordeaux region since the 18th century.

aperitif This is a word we have taken from the French meaning an alcoholic drink served before a meal. It can describe champagne, sherries and cocktails, but also applies to proprietary drinks such as *DUBONNET* and *CAMPARI*. These aperitifs are widely used in making cocktails, especially in Europe.

applejack An American apple brandy, made like the famous French CALVADOS, but matured for a shorter time.

apricot brandy Often a liqueur rather than a true brandy (that is, an infusion of apricots in brandy rather than being distilled from apricots as a true brandy would be).

armagnac see BRANDY.

Bacardi rum A clear or 'white' rum, made in Puerto Rico and an excellent cocktail mixer (see also RUM).

Bailey's Irish Cream A calorie-laden but low-alcohol Irish liqueur of chocolate-flavoured whiskey and double cream.

Bénédictine A famous French liqueur first made by the Bénédictine monks in the early 16th century. It is a unique blend of herbs, spices, blossoms and peels. The initials DOM on the bottle are the dedication *Deo Optimo Maximo* – 'To God Most Good, Most Great'.

bianco Italian for 'white', often used to describe the pale, medium sweet Italian VERMOUTH.

blackcurrant liqueur A dark, richly coloured, sweet blackcurrant and brandy liqueur. Also called CRÈME DE CASSIS.

bourbon American whiskey, distilled from corn or maize, first produced in Bourbon County, Kentucky. It lacks the subtlety of most Irish whiskeys and Scotch, but is a good mixer.

brandy The golden, honey-coloured spirit distilled from grapes is the most common brandy, but in fact any spirit distilled from fermented fruit juice is a brandy. Brandy varies enormously in taste and smoothness from the fiery (usually cheaper) types to the magnificent fine champagne *COGNACS* and armagnacs of France.

calvados The finest of the apple brandies, and one of the world's great liqueurs, this French brandy is a product of the Normandy region.

Campari An Italian aperitif, deep red in colour with a slightly bitter herb and quinine flavour.

champagne The finest of the sparkling white wines, made by the traditional *méthode champenoise*.

Chartreuse A French liqueur, made from over 130 herbs and spices, produced by the Carthusian monks for several centuries. Yellow and the more common and potent green Chartreuse are available.

cherry brandy Fruit is macerated in a brandy base to produce this brandy, which is really a cherry liqueur.

Cinzano A brand name for *VERMOUTH*.

Cointreau A renowned French liqueur, colourless, with an orange flavour, like a very fine *CURAÇAO*.

cognac The smooth, fine aged brandy from the French Cognac region. The initials, VSOP, on the label stands for 'Very Special Old Pale'.

crème de These words usually indicate a sweet brandy-based liqueur, though not necessarily with a creamy flavour or appearance.

crème de banane A pungent, banana liqueur.

crème de cacao Rich, very sweet cocoa and vanilla liqueur.

crème de cassis A dark, syrupy blackcurrant liqueur.

crème de fraises A red, strawberry-flavoured liqueur.

crème de framboise A delicately flavoured raspberry liqueur.

crème de menthe One of the best-known liqueurs, usually brilliant emerald green in colour (although a colourless version is sold) with a strong, sweet peppermint flavour.

crème de violette Fragrant liqueur with the exotic flavour and colour of violets.

curaçao A sweet, orange-flavoured liqueur widely used in cocktails. The driest curaçao is called *TRIPLE SEC*. Curaçao comes in orange, white (or clear), green, red and blue, although the flavour remains basically the same.

Drambuie A whisky liqueur made from scotch malt whisky and heather honey. The name Drambuie is Gaelic for 'the drink that satisfied'.

Dubonnet A French aperitif, deep red in colour with a quinine after-taste.

Fernet A bitter Italian aperitif, frequently drunk with soda water as a 'morning after' tonic.

fraises de bois A wild strawberry brandy liqueur.

Galliano A golden Italian liqueur, in a strikingly tall, narrow bottle. The distinctive flavour combines aniseed and vanilla.

gin Essential for any cocktail bar. A dry, colourless spirit distilled from grain and formulated in Holland in the 16th century, gin was originally made from juniper berries. The name is thought to be a corruption of the French word for juniper, *genièvre*. Dutch gin is also known as Hollands or Genever gin. The latter is still made in Holland. London Dry gin is a drier, more neutral spirit than the Dutch brew and is the style most widely made and used today. Plymouth gin was a more aromatic gin, distilled at Plymouth, to ensure a constant supply for British sailors. Plymouth gin is still the recommended spirit for PINK GIN even though it is no longer so full bodied.

ginger wine A fruit wine traditionally made from currants and powdered Jamaican ginger root.

Grand Marnier A justly famous orange-flavoured French cognac liqueur, first made in the 1880s.

grappa A type of brandy, often fiery and rather rough, which, in the Italian countryside, is frequently home-brewed.

grenadine A sugar syrup, pink in colour, flavoured with pomegranate. It is non-alcoholic, but a cocktail bar essential.

Guinness The famed Irish stout, a rich, dark malty brewed beer.

Kahlua A Mexican coffee liqueur flavoured with coffee beans and brandy.

kirsch A clear cherry brandy, which is distilled from black cherries.

Madeira A fortified wine, originally produced on the island of Madeira, off the Portuguese coast.

maraschino An Italian cherry liqueur made from marasca cherries and their kernels, giving it a delicate nutty flavour. Colourless and widely used in cocktails.

Midori A relatively new, luminous, green-coloured Japanese melon liqueur.

orange bitters A flavoursome, non-alcoholic essence, dry and bitter, often used in cocktails.

orgeat A non-alcoholic sweetened syrup, flavoured with almond, rose water and orange blossom.

ouzo Greek aniseed-flavoured spirit. Although clear in colour, when water is added it turns milky.

parfait amour A sweet, fragrant liqueur, pink or violet in colour, flavoured with citrus fruit, flower petals and spices.

peach brandy A soft, peach-flavoured liqueur.

Pernod An aniseed-flavoured French aperitif. Usually served only with water (like ouzo it turns cloudy).

Pimm's No 1 Cup A type of ready-mixed *GIN SLING*.

Piña Colada A rum-based liqueur with coconut cream and pineapple.

port Fortified wine from Portugal.

rum A distillation of sugar cane or molasses, produced in a range of styles (and colours) from white to golden and dark, and varying considerably in flavour and potency. The name *BACARDI* is synonymous with white rum, which has a much lighter flavour than many other rums and is a good cocktail mixer. Beware those labelled 'overproof', which are powerful indeed.

sambuca A clear, Roman liqueur resembling anisette.

sherry A fortified wine, originally produced in Spain in the district surrounding the town of Jerez. Usually drunk as an aperitif. The finest dry 'fino' sherries are served chilled.

Southern Comfort American liqueur, combining bourbon whiskey with peaches and a faint trace of orange. More like a spirit than a liqueur, being comparatively dry and potent.

sloe gin A liqueur made from sloes (a type of berry) macerated in gin. Traditionally served as the 'stirrup cup' before riding to hounds.

tequila A fiery Mexican spirit, distilled from the fermented mezcal plant. It is a very good cocktail base and has inspired many drinks.

Tia Maria A rum-based coffee-flavoured liqueur made in Jamaica.

triple sec A dry, colourless, highly refined *CURAÇAO*.

Van der Hum A tangerine-flavoured liqueur hailing from South Africa.

vermouth An aperitif made in France and Italy and available in dry, rosso (sweet) and bianco (medium sweet). It is a fortified aromatic wine, excellent served on ice, or as a cocktail base.

vodka A grain spirit, highly distilled, refined and colourless. Vodka, meaning 'little water', originated in Russia and Poland, but has become an international drink. Many of the Western vodkas are clear and virtually flavourless, making them an excellent base for cocktails.

whiskey, whisky Whisky (always spelt without the *e* in Scotland) is a grain spirit that can be served either straight or blended. Scotch whisky, made only in Scotland, is a blend of grains and malts and is best served by itself, or on the rocks, rather than mixed. Irish whiskey has more of a malt flavour and is a better mixer. Bourbon contains at least 51 per cent corn, and rye whiskey has at least 51 per cent rye; both are good mixers.

RECIPES

ADONIS ▼

60 ml dry sherry
30 ml sweet vermouth
2 dashes Angostura or orange bitters

Pour into a mixing glass with ice, stir well. Strain into a cocktail glass and add some fresh ice.

ALASKA ▼

A true cocktail – sophisticated, dry, potent, and the marvellous green colour of the French Chartreuse.

60 ml gin
15 ml (or less) green Chartreuse
lemon peel for twist
long spiral of lemon peel for garnish

Stir well in mixing glass with ice, then strain into a cocktail glass and add a twist of lemon. Drape the lemon peel over the glass rim.

ALGONQUIN ▮

Named in honour of one of New York's best-known hotels, so be sure to use American rye whiskey or bourbon.

60 ml bourbon
30 ml dry vermouth
30 ml pineapple juice

Shake well with ice, then strain into a glass and serve on the rocks.

AMBASSADOR ▮

60 ml tequila
30 ml sugar syrup
orange juice
orange slice for garnish

Pile ice cubes into an old-fashioned glass, add sugar syrup, tequila and orange juice. Stir gently. Decorate with an orange slice on the rim.

AMERICAN BEAUTY 🍸

20 ml brandy
20 ml dry vermouth
7 ml white crème de menthe
20 ml orange juice
dash of grenadine
30 ml port

Shake all the ingredients, except port, with ice. Strain into an old-fashioned glass, then slowly float the port on top.

AMERICAN FLYER 🍸

45 ml white rum
7 ml lime juice
pinch sugar
champagne
thin spiral of lime peel for garnish

Combine the rum, lime juice and sugar with ice and shake well. Strain into a glass, top with champagne. Hang the lime peel over the rim of the glass.

AMERICANO ▯

30 ml Campari
30 ml sweet vermouth
soda water
slice of orange for garnish

Fill an old-fashioned glass two-thirds full with ice, add Campari and vermouth, then top with soda water. Stir gently. Drop in a thin circle of orange and serve with a swizzle stick.

ANGEL FACE ▽

30 ml gin
30 ml apricot brandy
30 ml calvados
sliver of red apple (dipped in lemon juice) and red
   cherry for garnish

Shake with ice, strain into a chilled champagne saucer. Spear the apple and cherry with a toothpick and place on the rim of the glass.

APRICOT ANGEL* ▮

60 ml orange juice
10 ml lemon juice
pinch sugar
90 ml apricot nectar
dry ginger ale
cherry for garnish

Combine orange and lemon juice with sugar, stir to dissolve. Add apricot nectar. Top with dry ginger ale and ice blocks just before serving. Drop the cherry into drink and serve with a swizzle stick.

APRICOT PIE ▼

30 ml white rum
30 ml sweet vermouth
7 ml apricot brandy
½ teaspoon lemon juice
dash of grenadine
orange peel for twist

Shake all ingredients with ice. Strain into a cocktail glass, add a little ice and a twist of orange.

ATHOLL BROSE

This old Scottish drink was originally made with fine oatmeal, and was more a food than a drink. The modern version, containing cream, honey and whisky, is traditionally served at Hogmanay, the Scottish New Year celebrations.

45 ml Scotch whisky
45 ml clear honey
45 ml double cream

Warm a glass, then mix the ingredients well by stirring. Chill before serving.

B & B

30 ml brandy (or cognac if the occasion calls for it)
30 ml Bénédictine

Pour into a warmed brandy balloon, stir very gently and serve.

B 52

15 ml Kahlua
15 ml Cointreau
15 ml Bailey's Irish Cream

Pour liqueurs *in the above order* over the back of a spoon into a liqueur glass to create a layered effect.

BANANA COW $\Y$

The 'cow' is a modern cocktail, for those who enjoy the nourishment of dairy products with their spirits and liqueurs. The BROWN COW is another well-known cocktail.

30 ml white rum
30 ml crème de banane
45 ml cream
dash of grenadine
several slices of unpeeled banana (dipped in lemon
    juice) and grated nutmeg for garnish

Combine all ingredients in a cocktail shaker with ice. Shake well and strain into a cocktail glass. Make a cut in the banana slices and balance them on the rim. Dust the cocktail with nutmeg.

BARTENDER $\Y$

20 ml dry vermouth
20 ml sweet vermouth
20 ml gin
20 ml medium dry sherry
5 ml Grand Marnier
orange peel for twist

Stir all the ingredients in a mixing glass with ice. Strain into a cocktail glass or champagne saucer. Add a twist of orange and drop in the peel.

BEE'S KISS 🍸

45 ml white rum
1 teaspoon honey
1 teaspoon cream
cherry for garnish

Shake well with ice. Strain into an old-fashioned or cocktail glass. Garnish with a single cherry, if desired.

THE BELLINI 🍸

An Italian masterpiece, best made with fresh peaches, although you can use peach nectar.

champagne
1 fresh peach, peeled
a little castor sugar

Purée the peach and sugar in a blender. Pour into two chilled champagne flutes and top slowly with chilled champagne. Serves 2.

BETWEEN THE SHEETS 🍸

30 ml Cointreau
30 ml brandy
30 ml white rum
15 ml lemon juice
lemon peel for twist

Shake all ingredients with ice. Strain into your finest champagne saucer and add a twist of lemon.

BLACK EYE 🍸

45 ml vodka
10 ml blackberry brandy
40 ml lime juice
lime peel for twist

Combine ingredients with ice. Shake well and strain into a cocktail glass. Add a twist of lime and drop in the peel.

BLACK RUSSIAN 🍸

30 ml vodka
20 ml Kahlua
cola (optional)

Shake ingredients with ice, then strain into an old-fashioned or cocktail glass with fresh ice. Some drinkers like to top up with a dash of cola.

• Add a dash of lemon before shaking for a Black Magic.

BLACK VELVET 🥂

½ Guinness
½ dry champagne

Pour chilled ingredients into an elegant jug to mix, then decant into champagne flutes or pilsener glasses.

BLARNEY STONE   🍸

30 ml Irish whiskey
30 ml dry vermouth
30 ml green curaçao
3 dashes of orange bitters

Combine all ingredients with ice and shake well. Strain into a cocktail glass.

BLENDED COMFORT   ▯

45 ml bourbon
30 ml Southern Comfort
15 ml dry vermouth
30 ml orange juice
40 ml lemon juice
½ fresh peach, peeled
orange and lemon slices for garnish

Place all the ingredients into a blender with ice, blend on low speed for about 10 seconds. Strain into a chilled highball glass over cubes. Form the orange and lemon slices into twisted rings and rest on glass rim.

BLOOD AND SAND Y

30 ml sweet vermouth
30 ml Scotch whisky
30 ml cherry brandy
30 ml orange juice
sliver of orange peel for garnish

Shake well with ice and strain into a chilled champagne saucer. Drop the orange peel into the drink.

BLOODY MARY ▯

45 ml vodka
90 ml tomato juice
juice of ½ small lemon
few dashes each of Tabasco and Worcestershire sauce
salt and freshly ground black pepper (optional)
slice of lemon for garnish

Combine vodka, fruit juices and sauces with ice. Shake well and strain into a chilled highball glass with fresh ice. Float the lemon in the drink, and season with salt and pepper if desired.

• For a Bloody Maria use tequila in place of vodka.

BLUE BAYOU

30 ml gin
15 ml Galliano
15 ml dry vermouth
15 ml blue curaçao
lemonade
lemon slice and cherry for garnish

Combine all ingredients, except lemonade, with ice, and shake well. Strain into a glass, add ice cubes and lemonade. Garnish with lemon slice and cherry. Serve with a straw.

BLUE BLAZER

A cocktail for those who like to put on a show.

90 ml Scotch whisky
1 teaspoon castor sugar
90 ml boiling water
lemon peel for twist

Warm two mugs or heatproof glasses. Dissolve the sugar in the boiling water in one glass. Pour the scotch into the other and ignite. Then pour the Scotch and water from one mug to the other while flaming. When well mixed, pour into a warmed toddy glass. Allow to cool, add a twist of lemon and serve.

BLUE HAZE 🍸

15 ml parfait amour
15 ml dry vermouth
20 ml white rum
5 ml Cointreau

Pour the ingedients slowly *in this order* into a chilled cocktail glass. Place the glass in the refrigerator or freezer for about 5–10 minutes. The result is a pale frosty drink with a marvellous blue tinge at the base.

BLUE HEAVEN 🥛

30 ml white rum
15 ml blue curaçao
15 ml amaretto
15 ml fresh lime juice
75 ml pineapple juice
5 ml sugar syrup

Combine all ingredients and shake well. Strain into a highball glass with fresh ice.

BLUE LAGOON 🍸

30 ml vodka
30 ml blue curaçao
lemonade
cherry for garnish

Fill a highball glass two-thirds with ice, then add vodka, curaçao and lemonade. Garnish with a cherry and serve with swizzle stick and straw.

BOSOM CARESSER 🍸

One of the classic cocktails and hard to beat on a chilly winter's night. Madeira, the main ingredient, is a fortified wine. Despite this cocktail's bawdy name, Madeira was considered a very genteel drink during the Victorian era.

15 ml Madeira
7 ml brandy
7 ml orange curaçao
5 ml grenadine
1 egg yolk

Combine all ingredients with ice, and shake until frothy. Strain into a cocktail glass.

BOWLE ♟

90 ml brandy
90 ml triple sec or white curaçao
5 litres of white wine
2 dessertspoons sugar
fresh fruit (pineapples, peaches or strawberries)
1 bottle champagne

Place fruit in a bowl, add the brandy, liqueur and sugar. Leave for 5 hours or overnight. Add the wine and chill with ice blocks. Pour in the champagne just before serving.

BRANDY ALEXANDER ♟

60 ml brandy
30 ml crème de cacao
30 ml double cream
freshly-grated nutmeg for garnish

Shake ingredients well with ice. Strain into a cocktail glass and sprinkle lightly with nutmeg.

BRANDY CRUSTA ♆

30 ml brandy
30 ml orange curaçao
10 ml lemon juice
5 ml maraschino
spiral of lemon or orange peel for garnish

Sugar-frost the rim of a cocktail glass (see page 19), then place the spiral of peel into the glass. Shake all the ingredients well, strain into the prepared glass and serve.

- Fresh orange juice can be added for those drinkers who prefer a longer, softer drink.

BRANDY FLIP ♆

45 ml brandy
1 egg
1 teaspoon castor sugar
grated nutmeg for garnish

Shake all ingredients well with ice (or blend in a blender) and strain into a wine glass. Dust with nutmeg.

- Adding half a pint of milk will make a Brandy Egg Nog. Serve in a tall glass.

BRANDY HIGHBALL

30 ml brandy
dash of Angostura bitters
soda water or dry ginger ale
thin strip of lemon peel for garnish

Splash bitters into a highball glass, roll around, then shake out excess. Drop in some ice cubes, pour in the brandy and fill with soda water or dry ginger ale. Make a knot with the lemon peel and drop into drink.

BRONX

45 ml gin
15 ml dry vermouth
15 ml sweet vermouth
15 ml orange juice
15 ml lemon juice (optional)

Combine with ice, shake, strain into an old-fashioned glass and serve on the rocks.

BROWN COW

30 ml Kahlua
120 ml milk
grated nutmeg for garnish

Fill the glass with ice, then pour in the Kahlua and milk. Stir gently to mix and dust with nutmeg.

THE BUCK █

45 ml brandy
30 ml crème de menthe
7 ml fresh lemon juice
dry ginger ale
small cluster of seedless grapes for garnish

Combine brandy, crème de menthe and lemon juice with ice and shake well. Strain into a very tall glass and top with dry ginger ale. Hang the grapes on the rim of the glass.

BULLSHOT █

Regarded by many as one of the best 'morning after' restoratives.

45 ml vodka
120 ml beef bouillon
dash of Worcestershire sauce
dash of Tabasco sauce (optional)
20 ml lemon juice
salt and pepper
thick slice of lemon for garnish

In a mixing glass, mix all ingredients well with ice, strain into a highball glass, with a few ice cubes. Drop in the lemon.

BUNNY MOTHER $\Y$

45 ml vodka
15 ml lemon juice
15 ml orange juice
15 ml grenadine
5 ml Cointreau
$\frac{1}{4}$ of an orange slice and red cherry for garnish

Place all ingredients, except Cointreau, in a shaker with ice, and shake well. Strain into a glass, then float the Cointreau on top. Spear the orange and cherry with two toothpicks and balance across the top of the glass.

BUSHRANGER

30 ml Dubonnet
30 ml white rum
2 dashes of Angostura bitters
lemon peel for twist

Shake all the ingredients with ice. Strain into a chilled glass and add a twist of lemon.

CAPTAIN'S BLOOD 🔳

60 ml golden rum
30 ml fresh lime juice
few dashes of Angostura bitters
slice of lemon for garnish

Shake ingredients with crushed ice and strain into a chilled glass. Make a twisted ring with the lemon and drop into the drink.

CARA SPOSA 🍸

30 ml Tia Maria
30 ml orange curaçao
15 ml double cream

Blend at low speed in a blender with crushed ice for about 15 seconds. Strain into a cocktail glass and serve immediately.

CARIBBEAN SUNSET

An exotic cocktail with the brilliant colours and heady flavours of the tropics. If you enjoy decorating your drinks, this is the ideal cocktail. Serve in a generously sized brandy balloon or goblet.

30 ml gin
30 ml blue curaçao
30 ml crème de banane
30 ml fresh lemon juice
30 ml fresh cream
dash of grenadine
banana slivers (dipped in lemon juice) and cherries
   for garnish

Combine all the ingredients, except grenadine, and shake well. Strain into a glass. Add grenadine, which will sink to the bottom to create a 'sunset'. Alternate slivers of banana and whole cherries on a toothpick and rest on side of glass. Serve with straws.

CHAMPAGNE COCKTAIL

30 ml brandy
sugar cube
dash of Angostura bitters
champagne
quarter of an orange slice and strawberry for garnish

Place the sugar cube in a champagne saucer or flute and sprinkle with bitters. Add brandy then top with champagne. Rest the orange on the rim and drop the strawberry in the glass.

CHERRY BLOSSOM

45 ml brandy
15 ml cherry brandy
few drops curaçao
few drops grenadine
15 ml lemon juice
cherry brandy and castor sugar for frosting

Sugar-frost a cocktail glass, using cherry brandy and sugar (see page 19). Combine all ingredients with ice, shake well and strain into the glass.

CHIQUITA 🍸

45 ml vodka
10 ml crème de banane
10 ml lime juice
½ small banana, peeled and sliced
1 teaspoon castor sugar
banana slice (dipped in lemon juice) and cherry
  for garnish

Blend all ingredients with crushed ice at low speed until smooth. Strain into a champagne saucer. Make a cut in the banana slice and the cherry and rest them side by side on the rim. Serve immediately.

CINDERELLA* 🍸

40 ml orange juice
40 ml lemon juice
40 ml pineapple juice
orange and lemon slices for garnish

Combine the fruit juices with ice and shake well. Strain into a champagne saucer and place the fruit on the rim of the glass.

THE CLARIDGE ▼

30 ml gin
30 ml dry vermouth
15 ml apricot brandy
15 ml Cointreau or triple sec

Shake with ice and strain into a cocktail glass.

CLOVER CLUB ▼

Another sophisticated classic, with a traditional gin base and just a hint of sweetness, known to bartenders around the world.

45 ml gin
40 ml fresh lime juice
40 ml grenadine
egg white
spiral of lime peel for garnish

Shake all ingredients with ice. Strain into a frosty cold glass. Hang the lime peel over the edge of the glass, and serve immediately.

COFFEE FLIP 🍷

No coffee in the cocktail, but the ideal drink to serve after dinner with coffee.

45 ml cognac
30 ml port
30 ml sugar syrup
1 egg
grated nutmeg for garnish

Shake all ingredients well with ice. Strain into a small brandy glass, sprinkle with nutmeg and serve immediately.

COFFEE GRAND MARNIER 🍸

20 ml Grand Marnier
20 ml Kahlua
1 tablespoon fresh orange juice
orange slice for garnish

Pour liqueurs and orange juice into a mixing glass with ice and stir. Strain into a glass with a small scoop of crushed ice. Place the orange on the side of the glass.

COLADA CREAM COCKTAIL

60 ml Piña Colada
15 ml white rum
60 ml cream
slice of pineapple, pineapple leaves and a cherry
  for garnish

Shake well with ice and strain into a glass. Garnish with a triangle of pineapple, the tips of two pineapple leaves and a cherry, all secured with a toothpick.

CORPSE REVIVER

There are several variations of this cocktail, all of them potent and guaranteed to set you on the road to recovery.

30 ml brandy
15 ml calvados
15 ml sweet vermouth

Shake well with ice, strain into a glass and sip slowly.

CRAZY HORSE 🍸

20 ml Scotch whisky
10 ml strawberry liqueur
10 ml crème de banane
60 ml champagne
quarter of an orange slice and fresh mint leaves
    for garnish

Shake Scotch and liqueurs with ice. Strain into a champagne flute and top with champagne. Spear the orange and mint leaves on a toothpick and put on the edge of the glass.

CREOLE COOLER* 🥛

120 ml milk
60 ml crushed pineapple, chilled
20 ml orange juice
5 ml lime juice
castor sugar to taste
a long spear-shaped piece of pineapple for garnish

Blend milk, juices and sugar with ice in a blender and pour into a tall, chilled glass. Put the pineapple spear into the drink and serve with straws.

CUBA LIBRE

60 ml white rum
juice of one lime
cola

Pour the rum and lime juice into a tall glass, then add the spent lime shells, ice cubes and top with cola. Serve with a swizzle stick and straws.

DAIQUIRI

One of the great cocktails, created in Havana, made famous by Ernest Hemingway, and, naturally, made with rum. The classic version combines rum with lime, but there are endless fruity variations.

45 ml white rum
30 ml fresh lime juice (or lemon if you are desperate)
15 ml sugar syrup
lime peel for garnish

Shake well with ice and strain into a cocktail glass or champagne flute. Tie the peel into a knot, drop into the drink and serve immediately.

- Some versions use egg white, which makes a frothier drink. For a drier version, omit the sugar syrup.

Banana Daiquiri

45 ml white rum
30 ml Cointreau
45 ml cream
dash of banana liqueur
10 ml fresh lime juice
¾ fresh banana, sliced

Blend with ice until smooth, strain into a cocktail glass and serve immediately.

Cherry Daiquiri

45 ml white rum
20 ml cherry liqueur
10 ml fresh lime juice
few dashes of kirsch liqueur
lime peel for twist

Shake well with ice. Strain into a chilled glass with a little fresh ice and add a twist of lime.

Coconut Daiquiri

30 ml white rum
15 ml coconut liqueur
20 ml fresh lime juice
dash of egg white

Shake ingredients well with ice. Strain into a champagne saucer.

Daiquiri Blossom ▼

30 ml white rum
30 ml orange juice
dash of maraschino
spiral of orange peel for garnish

Shake well with ice, strain into a cocktail glass. Drape the orange peel over the rim of the glass.

Frozen Mango-lime Daiquiri ▼

45 ml white rum
20 ml lime liqueur
45 ml frozen mango nectar
slice of fresh mango for garnish

Blend all ingredients with ice on high speed for about 10 seconds. Pile into cocktail glass and decorate with mango.

Strawberry Daiquiri ▼

45 ml white rum
15 ml Cointreau
10 ml strawberry liqueur
5 ml fresh lime juice
10 fresh strawberries
strawberry for garnish

Blend all ingredients with ice, then strain into a cocktail glass. Serve with straws and garnish with a fresh strawberry.

DEATH IN THE AFTERNOON

Reputedly invented by Ernest Hemingway, and sometimes known simply as a Hemingway.

45 ml Pernod
champagne

Pour the Pernod into a chilled champagne flute, then slowly add champagne.

DIANA

A smooth, sweet after-dinner cocktail.

60 ml white crème de menthe
20 ml brandy or cognac

Pile crushed ice into a cocktail glass or small elegant wine glass. Add the crème de menthe, then float the brandy on top.

DUBONNET CASSIS

An aperitif, as only the French know how, using their fragrant blackcurrant liqueur, cassis.

60 ml Dubonnet
30 ml crème de cassis
sparkling water

Place several cubes of ice in an old-fashioned glass. Add Dubonnet and cassis, stir with a swizzle stick, then add a generous dash of sparkling water.

EAST INDIA

45 ml brandy
5 ml red curaçao
5 ml pineapple juice
2 dashes of Angostura bitters

Shake well with ice, then strain into a small wine glass and add a little fresh ice.

EGG NOG (HOT)

60 ml dark rum
30 ml milk
1 egg
2 teaspoons castor sugar
dash Angostura bitters

Gently heat the rum. Blend the other ingredients until smooth. Pour into warmed toddy glass, then add the rum. Stir and serve warm.

EL BURRO ♼

15 ml dark rum
15 ml Kahlua
30 ml coconut cream
30 ml double cream
½ banana, sliced
banana slices and cherry for garnish

Blend all ingredients with ice until smooth, then pour into a wine glass. Partially slit the banana and cherry and rest on rim of glass.

EL PRESIDENTE ♼

45 ml white rum
15 ml curaçao
15 ml dry vermouth
dash grenadine

Shake all ingredients well with ice. Strain into a cocktail glass, and add a little fresh, crushed ice.

EVE 🍸

A tempting cocktail, perfect as a late supper drink, best served in a champagne saucer or flute.

20 ml cognac
10 ml curaçao
2 teaspoons castor sugar
several dashes Pernod
pink champagne

Soak the sugar in the curaçao until dissolved. Swish Pernod around the champagne saucer. Add the cognac, then the sugar mixture. Stir gently, then slowly top with champagne.

FALLEN ANGEL 🍹

There is a Fallen Angel cocktail made with gin and crème de menthe, but this creamy pink advocaat version is very popular.

30 ml advocaat
40 ml cherry advocaat
lemonade
fresh ripe cherries (if in season) for garnish

Stir the two advocaats together in a tall glass. Add ice, then top with lemonade. Hang a pair of cherries over the side of glass. Serve with straw and swizzle stick.

FLUFFY DUCK

30 ml white rum
30 ml advocaat
lemonade
double cream
fresh strawberry for garnish

Mix the rum and advocaat in a highball glass with crushed ice. Top with lemonade, then float the cream on top. Cut the strawberry into a fan shape, rest on the edge of glass, and serve with a straw.

FRISCO SOUR

30 ml bourbon
30 ml Bénédictine
7 ml fresh lemon juice
7 ml fresh lime juice
lemon and lime slices for garnish

Shake all the ingredients well with ice. Strain into chilled glass. Twist the lemon and lime together, secure with a toothpick and balance on the rim.

FROSTY AMOUR 🍷

30 ml Southern Comfort
30 ml vodka
30 ml apricot brandy
5 ml parfait amour
dash of crème de banane
lemonade

Combine all ingredients, except the lemonade, with ice.
Shake, strain into a goblet or brandy balloon, then add
the lemonade slowly. Serve with swizzle stick.

GAUGUIN 🍸

A colourful tribute to artist Paul Gauguin's tropical
Tahitian days. Use fresh passion-fruit if possible.

60 ml white rum
10 ml passion-fruit syrup
10 ml fresh lime juice
10 ml fresh lemon juice
lime slice and cherry for garnish

Blend with ice until smooth. Strain into champagne
saucer and decorate with a twisted lime ring, positioning
the cherry in the middle of the toothpick.

GENOA ▯

20 ml sambuca
20 ml dry vermouth
45 ml grappa (or Italian brandy)
olive for garnish

Shake with ice and strain into a glass. Add a few ice cubes and an olive.

GIBSON Y

A fine example of how seriously Martini drinkers take their cocktails. A Gibson is a Dry Martini (see *MARTINI*) served with two white cocktail onions. To the *aficionado*, the difference is critical.

GIMLET Y

45 ml gin
10 ml lime cordial (Rose's Lime Cordial is
   recommended)
spiral of lime peel for garnish

Shake well with ice, strain into a chilled cocktail glass with a few small ice cubes and drop the lime peel into the drink.

- Some drinkers like a splash of soda, but don't overdo it!

GIN AND FRENCH 🍸

30 ml gin
30 ml dry vermouth
lemon slice for garnish

Pour straight into a short glass. Stir gently, add ice cubes
if desired and a lemon slice. Add a twist of lemon if you
like your drink drier still.

GIN AND IT 🍸

30 ml gin
30 ml sweet vermouth
orange slice for garnish

Pour the gin and vermouth into an old-fashioned glass.
Add a few ice cubes and float an orange slice in the drink.

GIN FIZZ

A Fizz should properly do just that – bubble and fizz. Some people view it as a pick-me-up before the serious cocktail drinking commences. If you add the soda from a siphon it's easier to get the extra sparkle. The classic is a Gin Fizz, but other spirits can be used.

60 ml gin
30 ml fresh lemon juice
15 ml lime juice (optional)
1 tablespoon castor sugar
soda water

Shake the gin, fruit juices and sugar with ice. Strain into a highball glass. Add soda and stir well to make a fizz. Serve immediately.

GIN SLING

A long, cool drink that earned its reputation beneath the slow-moving ceiling fans of Singapore's renowned Raffles Hotel, and other tropical venues.

60 ml gin
15 ml cherry brandy
15 ml lemon juice
1 teaspoon castor sugar (optional)
soda water
slice of lemon and red cherry for garnish

Shake the gin, brandy, juice and sugar well with ice. Strain into a tall glass, add an ice cube and top with soda. Form the lemon into a twisted ring on a toothpick with the cherry in the middle and balance across the top of the glass.

GLÜHWEIN

A spicy, hot mulled wine, especially popular in the ski lodges – but why wait for snow to enjoy yourself? Glühwein means 'glowing wine' and the drink was traditionally heated with a red-hot poker until it glowed.

1 bottle dry red wine
3 tablespoons sugar
2 slices orange
2 slices lemon
generous shake of powdered nutmeg
cinnamon stick
orange slices studded with cloves for garnish

Heat wine, fruit and spices in a saucepan until hot but not boiling. Stir until the sugar dissolves. Serve hot in mugs or toddy glasses, with a slice of orange in each glass. Serves 4.

• Some versions add a generous dash of brandy.

GOLDEN CADILLAC

30 ml Galliano
30 ml white crème de cacao
30 ml cream
strawberry for garnish

Shake well with ice and strain. Put the strawberry on rim of glass.

GOLDEN DREAM Y

20 ml Galliano
20 ml Cointreau
20 ml orange juice
20 ml cream

Shake well with ice and strain.

GRAND PASSION Y

60 ml gin
30 ml passion-fruit juice
2 dashes Angostura bitters

Shake with ice. Strain into a cocktail glass.

• White rum makes a good substitute for the gin.

GRASSHOPPER Y

30 ml green crème de menthe
30 ml white crème de cacao
30 ml single cream
red and green cherries for garnish

Shake well with ice. Strain into a frosty cold cocktail glass. Spear red and green cherries alternately on a toothpick and place across the top of the glass. Serve immediately.

• Add 30 ml of vodka for a Flying Grasshopper.

GREEN LADY 🍸

45 ml gin
15 ml green Chartreuse
15 ml yellow Chartreuse
7 ml fresh lime juice
lime slice and fresh mint leaves for garnish

Shake ingredients well with ice. Strain into a cocktail glass. Secure the lime and mint leaves with a toothpick and place on the rim.

HARVEY WALLBANGER 📱

One of the most called for mixed drinks in recent years, and certainly partly responsible for the wide reputation of the Italian liqueur Galliano.

60 ml vodka
20 ml Galliano
100–120 ml fresh orange juice
orange slices for garnish

Put the ice into a glass. Add vodka and orange juice, stir with a swizzle stick. Float Galliano on top and place the orange on the edge of the glass.

HIGHBALL

45 ml bourbon
dry ginger ale or soda water
lemon peel for twist

Put a generous quantity of ice cubes into a tall glass, add whiskey and top with dry ginger ale or soda water. Add a twist of lemon.

HIGHNOONER

30 ml vodka
15 ml apricot brandy
15 ml sherry
champagne

Pour vodka, brandy and sherry into a glass over ice. Top up with champagne.

HOT BUTTERED RUM

60 ml dark rum
1 teaspoon brown sugar
pinch each of cinnamon and nutmeg
60 ml boiling water
1 teaspoon butter
cinnamon stick

Put the sugar and spices in a warmed glass. Add boiling water and stir to dissolve sugar. Add rum, then float the butter on top. Serve with the cinnamon stick and drink while warm, as the butter melts.

HOT TODDY

60 ml Scotch whisky (or a spirit of your choice)
1 teaspoon honey
boiling water
lemon slice for garnish

Pour the whisky and honey into a glass, then add the boiling water, stirring to mix. Float the lemon slice and serve warm.

IRISH COFFEE

Not exactly a cocktail, but far too important – and popular – to omit. Although whiskey seems to have a special affinity with coffee, hence the famous Irish version, there are many excellent variations as listed below. Make sure the coffee is fresh and hot and that the cream covers the top.

45 ml Irish whiskey
fresh, strong black coffee
1 teaspoon sugar
double cream

Warm a toddy glass. Put the sugar in the base, then add whiskey and hot coffee, almost filling the glass, and stirring well. Float the cream on top.

- Calypso Coffee is made with Tia Maria.

- Caribbean Coffee with dark rum.

- Mexican Coffee with Kahlua.

- Monk's Coffee with Bénédictine.

- Normandy Coffee with calvados.

JAEGAR TEA

120 ml schnapps
120 ml rum
$\frac{1}{4}$ litre of water
juice of 1 orange or lemon
sugar to taste
1 tea bag

Bring all ingredients to the boil. Pour into heat-proof glasses and serve. Serves 2.

JAPANESE COCKTAIL

60 ml cognac
5 ml almond extract or orgeat
5 ml lime juice
dash of Angostura bitters
lime peel for twist
long spiral of lime peel for garnish

Shake well with ice, strain into a chilled cocktail glass. Add a twist of lime and drop the peel into the glass.

JAPANESE SLIPPER 🍸

30 ml Midori
30 ml Cointreau
30 ml lemon juice
sliver of honeydew melon for garnish

Combine with ice and shake well. Strain into champagne saucer. Garnish with fresh melon.

JELLY BEAN 🍹

30 ml ouzo
15 ml blue curaçao
15 ml grenadine
lemonade

Put a generous scoop of ice cubes into a tall glass, add ouzo, curaçao and grenadine. Stir well. Top with lemonade and serve with straws and swizzle stick.

KAMIKAZE 🍸

30 ml vodka
30 ml Cointreau
30 ml fresh lemon juice
5 ml lime cordial
sliver of lime peel for garnish

Shake well with ice. Strain into a cocktail glass or champagne saucer. Tie the peel into a loose knot, and drop into the drink.

KANGAROO Y

Sometimes called a Vodkatini, but either way, this drink is sure to get you hopping. It is dry and sharp.

45 ml vodka
20 ml dry vermouth
lemon peel for twist

Stir the vodka and vermouth in a mixing glass with ice, then strain into a cocktail glass. Add a twist of lemon.

KELLY'S COMFORT ▯

30 ml Southern Comfort
30 ml Bailey's Irish Cream
60 ml ice-cold milk
15 ml sugar syrup
3–4 fresh strawberries
fresh strawberry for garnish

Blend with a scoop of crushed ice until smooth and creamy. Pour into a chilled highball glass. Cut the strawberry to create a fan, then place on rim.

KIR ROYALE 🍾

The perfect aperitif, delicate in colour and flavour.

5–10 ml crème de cassis
dry champagne

Pour the cassis into your finest champagne flute, then top with champagne.

- A simple Kir uses a chilled dry white wine instead of champagne.

LAGUNA 🍸

60 ml Italian brandy
7 ml vodka
7 ml medium sweet vermouth
5 ml Campari
dash of orange bitters
red cherry for garnish

Shake well with ice and strain into a cocktail glass. Garnish this icy red drink by dropping a red cherry into the glass.

LAYER CAKE   ♟

This is a simpler version of the *POUSSE-CAFÉ*. Remember to float the ingredients one on top of the other by slowly pouring the drinks *in the order given*, either over the back of a spoon or into the bowl of a spoon to overflow.

30 ml crème de cacao
30 ml apricot brandy
30 ml double cream
red cherry for garnish

Pour *in this order* into a liqueur glass. Do not mix. Place a red cherry on top and chill before serving.

LOLITA   🍸

20 ml tequila
10 ml lime juice
1 teaspoon honey
2 dashes Angostura bitters

Shake with ice, strain into a cocktail glass and add one or two ice cubes.

LONG ISLAND ICED TEA 🍹

30 ml vodka
30 ml tequila
30 ml white rum
15 ml Cointreau
30 ml lemon juice
30 ml sugar syrup
dash of cola
long spiral of lemon peel

Build liquor ingredients over ice and add juice and syrup. Top with cola. Drop the peel into drink.

MAI TAI 🍹

A sweet tropical concoction, served around the world, but especially appropriate served 'pool-side'.

30 ml white rum
30 ml dark rum
15 ml orange curaçao
15 ml orgeat syrup or amaretto liqueur
juice of a fresh lime
pineapple spear, sliver of lime peel and fresh mint
    leaves for garnish

Half-fill a tall glass with ice. Squeeze in lime juice, then pour in the other ingredients. Stir with a swizzle stick. Slip the pineapple, lime and mint onto a toothpick, and serve with straws.

MANGO COCONUT CREAM*

150 ml mango nectar
100 ml coconut cream
150 ml apple juice
fresh strawberries for garnish

Blend juices and coconut cream with ice. Pour into highball glasses loaded with ice. Place several strawberries on the glass rim. Serves 2.

MANHATTAN

Like the classic MARTINI, a cocktail to master.

Sweet Manhattan
60 ml rye whiskey (some drinkers prefer bourbon)
30 ml sweet vermouth
cherry for garnish

Stir in a mixing glass with ice. Strain into a cocktail glass and drop in a single cherry.

- A Dry Manhattan uses dry vermouth instead of sweet and has a twist of lemon.

- A Perfect Manhattan contains both sweet and dry vermouth.

- A Rum Manhattan uses dark rum instead of whiskey.

MARGARITA Y

30 ml tequila
15 ml Cointreau or triple sec
10 ml fresh lime or lemon juice
lemon and salt for frosting

Salt-frost the rim of a cocktail glass (see page 19). Shake the ingredients well with ice, then strain into a cocktail glass.

MARTINI Y

The greatest of the classic cocktails; certainly the most talked about. The Martini is apparently simple and spartan in its ingredients, yet there are endless subtle variations, inspiring endless discourse (and disagreement).

The Martini is thought to have been invented for John D. Rockefeller, by a barman called Martini, at a New York hotel in about 1910.

The critical factor in a Martini is its dryness. The amount of vermouth to be added is the great question. Most agree, the less the better. Winston Churchill was said to measure his vermouth by glancing at the bottle (but never touching it) while pouring the gin. One barman is reputed to have let the shadow of the vermouth bottle fall across the gin. Others merely rinse the glass in vermouth before pouring the gin.

Classic (Dry) Martini ♟

45 ml gin
5 ml dry vermouth
lemon peel for twist
olive for garnish (optional)

Stir the gin and vermouth with ice cubes in a mixing glass until just chilled. Quickly strain into a chilled glass. Add a twist of lemon (but not the peel) and an olive (if you must).

- For a Sweet Martini, use sweet vermouth.

- A Perfect Martini contains both sweet and dry vermouth.

MELON FRAPPÉ ♟

A frappé is a refreshing icy cocktail, almost like a sorbet. You can use any liqueur, but melon is especially right for summer.

45 ml melon liqueur
crushed ice
balls of fresh melon

Pile a scoop of crushed ice into a cocktail glass and drench with the liqueur. Spear melon balls on a tooth-pick and rest inside the glass. Serve with short straws.

MERRY WIDOW Y

45 ml Dubonnet
45 ml dry vermouth
lemon peel for twist (optional)

Pour into a mixing glass and stir with ice. Strain into a cocktail or old-fashioned glass. Add a few ice cubes, and a twist of lemon, if you like.

MEURICE Y

30 ml vodka
30 ml crème de banane
30 ml double cream
banana slivers (dipped in lemon juice) and a sprig of
    fresh mint for garnish

Shake well with ice. Strain into a champagne saucer. Join the banana and mint with a toothpick and place on the rim.

MIMOSA ♀

10 ml orange curaçao
30 ml fresh orange juice
60 ml champagne

Pour the juice and liqueur into a champagne flute and top with curaçao.

- Just the champagne and orange juice makes a Buck's Fizz.

MINT JULEP

60 ml bourbon
1 teaspoon castor sugar
4–5 fresh mint leaves
soda water
sprig of fresh mint for garnish

Muddle the mint leaves and sugar in the base of a tall glass to crush the sugar and release the flavour and aroma of the mint. Add the bourbon and stir until the sugar dissolves. Then clink in some ice cubes, top with soda water, add the mint leaves for garnish and serve.

MOCHA MINT

A smooth, after-dinner cocktail to serve with coffee.

30 ml Kahlua
30 ml white crème de menthe
30 ml white crème de cacao

Shake with ice, then strain into a glass and serve on the rocks.

MONTANA

30 ml brandy
30 ml dry vermouth
10 ml port

Stir in a mixing glass with ice until chilled. Pour into an old-fashioned glass with one cube of ice.

MORNING GLORY

30 ml brandy
15 ml orange curaçao
dash of Pernod
15 ml fresh lemon juice
dash of Angostura bitters
soda water
lemon peel for twist

Combine all ingredients, except soda water, with ice, shake well, strain into a glass and top with soda water. Add a twist of lemon.

MOSCOW MULE

40 ml vodka
20 ml fresh lime juice
ginger beer
long sliver of cucumber peel and lime slice for garnish

Pile ice into a tall glass, add vodka, lime juice and top up with ginger beer, then stir. Put the cucumber peel in the drink and fix the lime to the edge of the glass. Serve with straws.

NEGRONI 🍸

30 ml Campari
30 ml sweet vermouth
30 ml gin
lemon peel for twist

Shake well with ice. Strain into a wine glass over ice cubes and add a twist of lemon.

- For a longer, sweeter drink, omit the lemon, top with soda and add a slice of orange.

OLD FASHIONED ▮

This American classic should be made with an American whiskey, either a bourbon or a rye.

60 ml bourbon or rye whiskey
10 ml sugar syrup
2 dashes of Angostura bitters
soda water
lemon peel for twist
orange slice and a cherry for garnish

Mix the sugar syrup and bitters in an old-fashioned glass. Add the whiskey, a few large ice cubes, a splash of soda water and twist of lemon. Form a twisted ring with the orange and cherry. Place on the rim.

OLE 🍷

A tequila drink guaranteed to make you toss your sombrero in the sky.

45 ml tequila
30 ml Kahlua
20 ml sugar syrup
double cream

Mix tequila, Kahlua and sugar syrup in a mixing glass. Strain into a cocktail glass with a little crushed ice. Float the cream on top.

ONE IRELAND 🍷

30 ml Irish whiskey
15 ml crème de menthe
1 scoop vanilla ice-cream
green maraschino cherries for garnish

Blend with a scoop of crushed ice until just smooth. Pour into a cocktail glass, spear two or three cherries on a toothpick and place in the glass. Serve immediately with short straws.

ORANGE BLOOM ♙

30 ml gin
10 ml Cointreau
10 ml sweet vermouth
long spiral of orange peel for garnish

Shake well with ice, strain into a well-chilled glass. Hang the spiral of peel over the rim.

ORANGE BLOSSOM ♙

30 ml gin
10 ml orange curaçao
30 ml fresh orange juice
half an orange slice for garnish

Shake well with ice. Strain into a wine glass with a little crushed ice and put the orange slice on the edge of the glass.

ORANGE FIZZ

60 ml gin
10 ml triple sec or Cointreau
15 ml orange juice
15 ml lemon juice
1½ teaspoons castor sugar
2 dashes orange bitters
soda water
orange slice for garnish

Shake all ingredients, except the soda water, with ice.
Strain into a wine goblet. Add ice cubes then soda water,
while stirring. Float the orange slice.

ORGASM

30 ml Cointreau
30 ml Bailey's Irish Cream

Build over ice.

PANSY

30 ml Pernod
5 ml grenadine
2 dashes Angostura bitters

Pour into a cocktail shaker with ice and shake well.
Strain into a frosty cold cocktail glass.

PEACH VELVET 🍸

45 ml peach brandy
15 ml white crème de cacao
15 ml double cream
fresh mint leaves and strawberry for garnish

Blend with a small scoop of crushed ice until creamy and smooth. Pour into a chilled glass. Join the mint leaves and strawberry on a toothpick and balance across the top of the glass.

PIMM'S 🍺

Pimm's No. 1 Cup is a ready-made cocktail, a blend of liqueurs and herbs with a gin base. It is best as a long cool drink with lemonade or other soft drink, a generous amount of ice and a fruit garnish.

90 ml Pimm's No. 1 Cup
soft drink (lemonade, soda water or dry ginger ale)
slices of cucumber peel, orange and lemon for garnish

Pile ice into a tall glass. Add Pimm's and soft drink (half soda water, half lemonade is a good combination). Drop cucumber peel into the drink, rest orange and lemon slices on the rim.

- A jug of Pimm's is an easy way to make a punch for a summer luncheon.

PIÑA COLADA 🍸

There is a ready-mixed liqueur on the market called Piña Colada, but here is how to make your own fruity coconut drink.

60 ml white rum
30 ml coconut cream
120 ml pineapple juice
long spear-shaped piece of pineapple, and a cherry
   for garnish.

Blend with a scoop of crushed ice until smooth. Pour into a highball glass with ice cubes. Make a slice in the pineapple and cherry and place them side by side on the rim.

PINEAPPLE PARADISE* 🍸

120 ml pineapple juice
40 ml lemon juice
30 ml sugar syrup
1 egg white
40 ml iced water
cherry for garnish

Blend at high speed until frothy. Pour into a tall chilled glass, garnish with a cherry. Serve immediately.

PINK GIN 🍸

Famed for its health-giving properties throughout the British Empire, Pink Gin was devised to make medicinal Angostura bitters more palatable for British seamen. Plymouth gin, originally distilled at the naval port of Plymouth to ensure a steady supply of gin for the navy is best for Pink Gin. Traditionally drunk tepid or at room temperature – add a dash of ice or iced water if you prefer a colder drink.

45 ml Plymouth gin (or dry gin, at a pinch)
several dashes of Angostura bitters
iced water (optional)

Pour the bitters into a glass, roll around to coat the sides, then tip out any excess. Pour in the gin. Add a little ice or a splash of iced water, if you like.

PINK PANTHER 🍸

45 ml vodka
30 ml bourbon
30 ml coconut cream
30 ml cream
10 ml grenadine
desiccated coconut and maraschino cherry for garnish

Blend at low speed with crushed ice, then pour into a chilled wine glass. Dip the cherry into the coconut until coated, then place on the rim of the glass.

PINK PUSSY ◼

30 ml Campari
15 ml peach brandy
dash of egg white
bitter lemon soft drink

Shake the Campari, peach brandy and egg white with ice until frothy. Strain into a glass with several ice cubes and top with bitter lemon.

PLANTER'S PUNCH ◼

Another drink with endless permutations – the only constant is a generous quantity of rum. White or gold rum can be used, though the slightly darker rum has a stronger flavour.

60 ml gold or white rum
30 ml fresh lime juice
30 ml orange juice
5 ml sugar syrup
5 ml grenadine
soda water
orange slice for garnish

Fill a highball glass two-thirds with ice, then build the ingredients into the glass. Pour in soda water and stir. Add the orange slice and serve with straws to sip languidly as you survey the plantation – or at least dream about it.

POM POM* ▯

A frivolous pink cocktail for those 'on the wagon'.

30 ml fresh lemon juice
½ egg white
5 ml grenadine
lemonade
cherry for garnish

Shake all except the lemonade until frothy. Strain into a glass, add a few ice cubes and top slowly with lemonade (so that it doesn't overflow). Float a cherry on top and serve with straws.

POUSSE-CAFÉ 🍸

Layered cocktails are a bartender's trick of the trade and are well worth mastering, particularly if you have a well-stocked cocktail cabinet and like to impress friends. The liqueurs must be poured in very slowly over the back of a spoon, *in the order given*, so that each floats on top of the other. There are various combinations of liqueurs, but here is one colourful creation. It is best to use a straight-sided liqueur glass.

10 ml grenadine
10 ml maraschino
10 ml green crème de menthe
10 ml crème de violette
10 ml green Chartreuse
10 ml brandy or cognac

Pour the liqueurs over the back of a spoon into the glass, *in the above order*. Do not stir. A straight-sided glass is needed.

P.S. I LOVE YOU 🥃

30 ml Kahlua
30 ml amaretto
30 ml Bailey's Irish Cream

Clink several cubes of ice into a short glass, top with liqueurs and stir.

PUSSY FOOT* 🍷

A non-alcoholic cocktail that looks as exotic as anything laced with liquor.

60 ml fresh orange juice
30 ml fresh lemon juice
5 ml grenadine
½ egg yolk
fresh cherries for garnish

Shake well with ice. Strain into a generous wine glass. Hang two fresh cherries over the side as a garnish and serve with straws.

RED EYE 🍷

120 ml lager
120 ml tomato juice

Pour both into a chilled pilsener or highball glass at the same time, and here's looking at you.

RED ROOSTER 🍷

45 ml vodka
30 ml fraises de bois
lemon peel for twist

Put several ice cubes into a short glass, then pour in vodka and liqueur and add a twist of lemon. Serve with short straws.

THE RICKEY ▯

Most versions of a 'Rickey' are flavoured with lime, although the spirit base may change. Like so many other cocktails the original was gin-based, but whisky is now popular.

60 ml whisky (bourbon is fine)
45 ml fresh lime juice
dash of grenadine
soda water
spiral of lime peel

Pour the whisky, lime juice and grenadine into an old-fashioned glass with a few ice cubes and stir. Add a little soda water and drop in the lime peel.

RITZ FIZZ ▯

An elegant drink with an evocative name for those 'putting on the Ritz' or perhaps just dreaming about it.

dash of amaretto
dash of blue curaçao
5 ml strained lemon juice
champagne
rose petal for garnish

Pour the amaretto, curaçao and lemon juice into a champagne flute, then slowly add the champagne. The traditional garnish is a fresh rose petal, floated on top.

ROB ROY 🍸

30 ml Scotch whisky
30 ml sweet vermouth
dash of Angostura bitters
cherry for garnish

Stir with ice in a mixing glass, then strain into a goblet with extra ice. Drop a cherry into the glass.

RUBY FIZZ 🍸

60 ml sloe gin
5 ml lemon juice
1 teaspoon castor sugar
few dashes of grenadine
1 egg white
soda water

Shake all but the soda water well with ice. Strain into a wine glass and add soda water.

RUSSIAN ESPRESSO 🍸

45 ml vodka
20 ml espresso coffee liqueur
lemon peel for twist

Shake well with crushed ice. Strain into a chilled glass and add a twist of lemon.

RUSTY NAIL 🍸

30 ml Scotch whisky
20 ml Drambuie
lemon peel for twist (optional)

Pour into an old-fashioned glass and serve on the rocks.
Add a twist of lemon, if you must.

SALTY DOG 🍸

60 ml vodka
fresh grapefruit juice
salt and lemon for frosting
long sliver of grapefruit peel for garnish

Salt-frost the rim of an old-fashioned glass (see page 19).
Pour vodka onto three or four ice cubes, then top with
grapefruit juice. Tie the grapefruit peel into a knot, and
drop into the glass.

SANGRIA   🍷

A punch rather than a cocktail, but an excellent summer party drink. If you wish to be authentic, you could use a dry Spanish wine.

1 bottle dry red wine
60 ml brandy
30 ml curaçao
30 ml orange juice
$\frac{1}{4}$ cup castor sugar
orange and lemon slices, halved

Put ice and fruit slices into a large jug. Add the other ingredients and stir well. Serve in generously sized wine glasses.

• Some versions add soda water just before serving.

SCREWDRIVER   🥃

45 ml vodka
60 ml orange juice
slice of orange for garnish

Pour the vodka then the juice into a glass with ice cubes and stir. Cut the slice of orange in half and fix both pieces to the side of the glass.

• For a Comfortable Screw add 30 ml Southern Comfort.

SHERRY FLIP   🍸

45 ml medium sherry
3 dashes crème de cacao
1 teaspoon castor sugar
1 egg
freshly grated nutmeg for garnish

Blend with a small scoop of crushed ice until smooth. Strain into a chilled cocktail glass and dust with nutmeg. Serve immediately.

SHIRLEY TEMPLE*   🥛

dry ginger ale
few dashes grenadine
cherry for garnish

Pile ice into a highball glass, then add grenadine and dry ginger ale. Decorate with a cherry and serve with a swizzle stick and straw.

SIDECAR   🍸

60 ml brandy (or cognac)
7 ml Cointreau
7 ml lemon juice
spiral of lemon peel for garnish

Shake well with ice and strain into a cocktail glass. Put the spiral of lemon peel in the drink.

- For a Boston Sidecar add 30 ml white rum.

SILVER FIZZ 🍸

20 ml gin
30 ml fresh lemon juice
10 ml sugar syrup
1 egg white
40 ml soda water

Shake all ingredients, except soda water, until frothy.
Strain into a frosty cold glass and top with soda water.

SILVER SUNSET 🍸

20 ml vodka
10 ml apricot brandy
10 ml Campari
10 ml fresh orange juice
10 ml fresh lemon juice
dash of egg white
fresh cherries and orange slice for garnish

Shake with ice, then strain into a cocktail glass. Put the
orange slice on the rim and hang the cherries over the
side.

SNOWBALL 🍸

45 ml advocaat
90 ml lemonade
strawberry for garnish

Pour the advocaat into a large wine glass, then slowly add the lemonade while stirring. Float the strawberry on top and serve with straws.

SOUTH PACIFIC ▯

30 ml gin
20 ml Galliano
20 ml blue curaçao
lemonade
lemon slice and blue cocktail cherry for garnish

Fill a highball glass two-thirds with ice. Add gin and Galliano then lemonade. Pour in blue curaçao, which will sink to the bottom, creating a layered effect. Use a toothpick to secure the lemon and cherry and balance across the top of the glass.

SPRITZER 🍷

60 ml chilled white wine
soda water

Pour into a chilled white-wine glass.

STINGER 🍸

45 ml brandy, Scotch whisky or other spirit
20 ml white crème de menthe

Shake the spirit and liqueur with ice, then strain into a glass and serve on the rocks.

STRAWBERRY DAWN 🍸

30 ml gin
30 ml coconut cream
4 strawberries
fresh strawberry and slice of kiwi fruit for garnish

Blend the gin and coconut cream with strawberries and crushed ice in a blender. Pour into a champagne saucer or cocktail glass. Decorate with strawberry and kiwi fruit.

SUNDOWNER 🍸

20 ml brandy
10 ml Van der Hum liqueur
10 ml lemon juice
10 ml orange juice

Stir with ice in a mixing glass and strain into a chilled cocktail glass.

TEQUILA FRESA Y

45 ml tequila
15 ml strawberry liqueur
10 ml lime juice
dash of orange bitters
$\frac{1}{4}$ of a slice of lime and strawberry for garnish

Shake well with ice. Strain into a frosty cold cocktail glass. Secure the lime and strawberry with a toothpick and place on the side of the glass.

TEQUILA SOUR Y

45 ml tequila
15 ml fresh lemon juice
dash of grenadine or 7 ml sugar syrup
half a slice of lemon for garnish

Shake with ice and strain into a cocktail glass. Drop the lemon into the drink.

TEQUILA SUNRISE ▯

60 ml tequila
10 ml grenadine
100 ml orange juice

Pour the tequila over ice cubes into a tall glass, then add orange juice. Pour the grenadine in last, so that it sinks to the bottom to create a 'sunrise'.

TOM COLLINS

A Collins should be long, laced with alcohol but not too strong, with a generous dash of lemon or lime and plenty of ice and soda. A Tom Collins is the classic, but don't let that put you off the many thirst-quenching variations.

60 ml gin
45 ml lemon juice
7 ml sugar syrup
soda water
lemon peel for twist (optional)

Combine gin, juice and sugar syrup in a very tall highball glass. Stir well, add ice and top with soda water. Add a twist of lemon, if you wish.

- A Jack Collins uses apple brandy.

- A Mike Collins uses Irish whiskey.

- A Pedro Collins uses rum.

- A Pierre Collins uses cognac.

- A Sandy Collins uses Scotch whisky.

TOMATO COCKTAIL*

240 ml tomato juice
100 g thinly sliced carrots
2 dashes Tabasco sauce
pinch of salt, freshly ground pepper
slice of lemon for garnish

Blend with crushed ice until well mixed. Strain into tall glasses and serve on the rocks, with lemon and straws. Serves 2.

TRINIDAD

30 ml crème de cacao
cola

Put ice into an old-fashioned glass, then liqueur and top with cola.

VIVA MEXICO

30 ml tequila
20 ml white crème de cacao
20 ml Midori
30 ml pineapple juice
30 ml orange juice
¼ slice of pineapple and cherry for garnish

Shake well with a scoop of crushed ice. Pour into a balloon glass. Make slits in the pineapple and cherry and balance on the glass's edge.

VODKA SOUR Y

45 ml vodka
15 ml fresh lemon juice
15 ml sugar syrup
cherry for garnish

Shake with crushed ice. Strain into a glass and decorate with a single cherry on the rim of the glass.

WHISKY COBBLER ▉

45 ml Scotch whisky
10 ml grapefruit juice
20 ml lemon juice
7 ml almond extract
cherry for garnish

Pour into an old-fashioned glass. Stir well, then add several cubes of ice. Drop the cherry into the drink.

WHISKY MAC ▉

60 ml Scotch whisky
60 ml ginger wine

Shake with ice. Serve on the rocks in a short glass.

WHISKEY SOUR 🍸

60 ml bourbon or rye whiskey
20 ml lemon juice
1 teaspoon castor sugar
1 teaspoon egg white (optional)
slice of lemon for garnish

Shake with ice, then strain into a chilled cocktail glass.
Place lemon slice on the rim and serve immediately.

WHITE GOLD 🥃

30 ml crème de banane
30 ml Galliano
30 ml apricot nectar
30 ml pineapple juice
½ egg white
banana slice and cherry for garnish

Blend ingredients with a scoop of crushed ice until
smooth and frothy. Pour into a tall glass. Spear the
banana and cherry together on a toothpick and rest
across the top of the glass.

WHITE LADY 🍸

45 ml Cointreau
10 ml brandy or cognac
10 ml white crème de menthe

Shake with ice, strain into a cocktail glass or champagne saucer.

WHITE RUSSIAN ▯

30 ml Kahlua
30 ml vodka
30 ml fresh cream

Pour into a chilled glass with ice cubes and stir. Serve with a swizzle stick and short straws.

WIDOW'S KISS 🍸

30 ml calvados
10 ml Bénédictine
10 ml yellow Chartreuse
dash of Angostura bitters
fresh strawberry for garnish

Stir in a mixing glass with ice, then strain into a cocktail glass. Cut the strawberry to create a fan, then place on the side of the glass.

YOGHURT FRUIT FROTH* 🍹

1 cup plain yoghurt
120 ml fresh orange-juice concentrate
120 ml pineapple juice
orange slices for garnish

Blend for about 10 seconds until frothy. Pour into chilled glasses with ice cubes. Form two orange slices into twisted rings with a toothpick and place on each glass rim. Serves 2.

ZOMBIE 🍹

45 ml golden rum
20 ml white rum
20 ml dark rum
5 ml overproof rum
15 ml each of pineapple, lime and grapefruit juice
1 teaspoon castor sugar
mint leaves and fresh fruit for garnish

Blend all, except the overproof rum, with a scoop of crushed ice. Pour into a highball glass and float the overproof rum on top. Garnish with fresh fruit and mint leaves.

INDEX